Dear Parent:
Your child's love of reading starts here!

Every child learns to read in a different way and at his or her own speed. You can help your young reader improve and become more confident by encouraging his or her own interests and abilities. You can also guide your child's spiritual development by reading stories with biblical values and Bible stories, like I Can Read! books published by Zonderkidz. From books your child reads with you to the first books he or she reads alone, there are I Can Read! books for every stage of reading:

 SHARED READING
Basic language, word repetition, and whimsical illustrations, ideal for sharing with your emergent reader.

 BEGINNING READING
Short sentences, familiar words, and simple concepts for children eager to read on their own.

 READING WITH HELP
Engaging stories, longer sentences, and language play for developing readers.

 READING ALONE
Complex plots, challenging vocabulary, and high-interest topics for the independent reader.

 ADVANCED READING
Short paragraphs, chapters, and exciting themes for the perfect bridge to chapter books.

I Can Read! books have introduced children to the joy of reading since 1957. Featuring award-winning authors and illustrators and a fabulous cast of beloved characters, I Can Read! books set the standard for beginning readers.

A lifetime of discovery begins with the magical words **"I Can Read!"**

Visit www.icanread.com for information on enriching your child's reading experience.
Visit www.zonderkidz.com for more Zonderkidz I Can Read! titles.

MADE BY GOD

CURIOUS CREATURES

ZONDERKIDZ

Curious Creatures
Copyright © 2014 by Zonderkidz
Photos © 2014 by Shutterstock

This title is also available as a Zondervan ebook.
Visit www.zondervan.com/ebooks.

Requests for information should be addressed to:

Zonderkidz, 3900 *Sparks Drive, Grand Rapids, Michigan 49546*

ISBN 978-0-310-73119-1

Editor: Mary Hassinger
Cover and interior design: Cindy Davis

Printed in China

14 15 16 17 18 /CTC/ 10 9 8 7 6 5 4 3 2 1

TABLE OF CONTENTS

RAIN FOREST FRIENDS

Rain forests cover only about 6% of the earth, but more than 1/2 of the world's plants and animal species live there.

There are 2 kinds
of rain forests:

- temperate rain forests—
found along coastlines
and have long wet
winters and springs and
a dry summertime.

- tropical rain forests—
found around the
equator. It is very hot
and wet all year.

ANACONDA!

The scientific name of the green anaconda is *Eunectes murinus*. *Eunectes* comes from a Greek word for "good swimmer".

A group of anaconda is called a "group" or "knot".

The anaconda is the
largest snake in the world.
The longest known anaconda
was 37.5 feet long!
An anaconda can weigh 550 pounds
and be as big around
as a grown man.

Most anacondas
are found in the
areas along the
Amazon and
Orinoco rivers.

Babies measure
2 feet long at birth
and take care of
themselves from
the start.

Anaconda eyes and nostrils are on top of their heads, so they can keep their body hidden underwater as they wait for prey.

The green anaconda can stay underwater for as long as 10 minutes without coming to the surface to breathe.

Most anacondas are found in swampy, tropical areas in South America.

They like to be in water.

They live alone and can live for ten or more years.

They also like to eat wild pigs, deer, birds, turtles, capybaras, caimans, and jaguars.

God put anacondas on earth for a good reason.

They hunt and eat many animals that could become pests, like rodents and deer.

Humans are the anaconda's most dangerous predator.

Anacondas hunt at night.

When they catch their food they squeeze it until it stops breathing.

Then the snake swallows it whole.

If the dinner is big, the anaconda doesn't need to eat again for a long time.

An anaconda can also be called a water boa.

Some people hunt anacondas and use the snakeskins to make clothing.

God made anacondas big and strong.

He made another animal from the rain forest big and strong.

He made the …

BENGAL TIGERS

Bengal tigers are also known as Indian tigers.

Bengal tigers are the most common tiger in the world—about one-half of all tigers in the world are Bengal tigers.

Some Bengal tigers range through Napal, Bangladesh, Bhutan, and Myanmar.

Bengal tigers can be found

in the tropical forests of India.

They are big cats that like to swim!

The Bengal tiger runs

very fast too.

Hearing is the tiger's sharpest sense, five times better than humans.

Bengal tigers live on average 15 years in the wild and 20+ in captivity.

The Bengal tiger can grow very big. They can be four-and-a-half to ten feet long and weigh 500 pounds.

These big tigers have to eat a lot. They catch animals like buffalo and wild pigs using their good nighttime vision, huge teeth, and claws.

One tiger can eat up to 60 pounds of meat at one time!

Foods the tiger likes are young elephants, monkeys, birds, frogs, and porcupines.

A Bengal tiger's night vision is six times stronger than a human's.

Females give birth to litters of 2 to 6 cubs.

Cubs cannot hunt until they are 18 months old and remain with their mothers for 2 to 3 years.

Bengal tigers like to be alone.

They sleep for up to eighteen hours a day!

But some live in small groups called streaks.

The Bengal tiger's roar is loud.

It can be heard up to

two miles away!

Tigers use their **distinctive coats as camouflage (no two have exactly the same stripes).**

There are rare white Bengal tigers that have white and black striped coats and blue eyes.

Bengal tiger body parts are used in traditional Chinese medicine.

All species of tigers in the world are considered endangered.

If people do not start taking care of God's world, the Bengal tigers might not survive.

Another rain forest creature that people must care for is the special …

SPIDER MONKEY!

Some people keep spider monkeys as pets.

Logging, hunting, and habitat destruction have made the spider monkey an endangered species.

There are fourteen kinds
of spider monkeys.

These monkeys live in the
upper layer of the rainforests
in Central and South America.

Some of these spider monkeys are called:

Red-faced spider monkey

White-front spider monkey

Mexican spider monkey

Spider monkeys do not always coexist well with humans.

They can be noisy animals and communicate with many calls, screeches, barks, and other sounds.

Spider monkeys gather in groups of up to two- or three-dozen animals.

Foraging for food occurs in smaller groups, and is usually most intense early in the day.

Spider monkeys live in groups called troops. They love to eat fruit. They also like leaves, flowers, and bugs.

The spider monkey's brain is bigger than most monkeys'. This large brain helps them remember where to find good food in the rainforest.

A spider monkey's brain weighs 107 grams or 3.77 ounces.

Spider monkeys can live
for 20 or more years.
They do not get too big—
they might be 14–26 inches long
and weigh 21–24 pounds.
Spider monkeys have four fingers
and no thumbs!

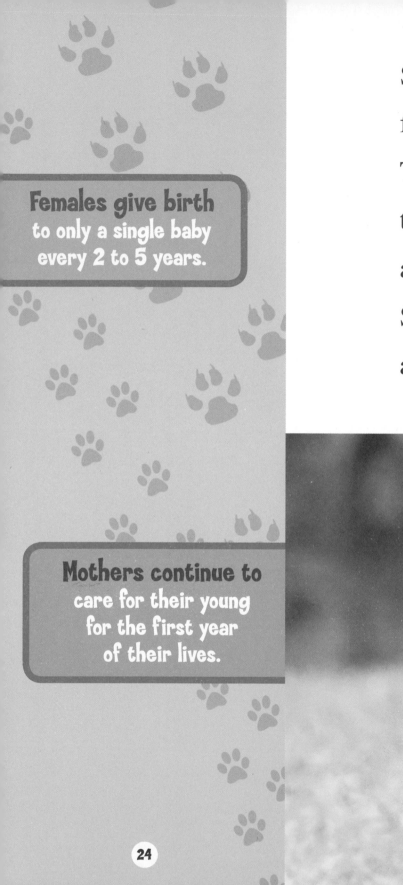

Females give birth
to only a single baby
every 2 to 5 years.

Mothers continue to
care for their young
for the first year
of their lives.

God gave spider monkeys long tails to help them hold branches as they swing around trees. God makes sure that all of his creatures have what they need to live, just like thc …

A spider monkey's tail accounts for about 60% of its length.

It's been recorded that with one swing of the arm, a spider monkey can cover 40 feet.

TOUCANS!

Toucans are very popular pets, and many are captured for this reason. They are also familiar commercial mascots.

The color of the toucan bill can be black, blue, brown, green, red, white, yellow, or a combination of colors.

Their bright colors actually provide good camouflage in the light of the rain forest canopy.

A toucan's bill can measure up to 8 inches in length.

The toucan has a huge bill! It can be very colorful and can grow to be 1/3 of the toucan's length.

A toucan's bill is not solid material but similar to a honeycomb, so is very light.

A toucan's average life span in the wild is up to 20 years.

The toucan uses its long bill to get fruit, bird eggs, bugs, and other food.

They eat fruit whole and spit the seeds out—that helps more trees grow!

Toucans live in the rainforests of South America. They build their nests in hollow tree parts.

The rainbow-billed toucan is the national bird of Belize.

There are about 40 different kinds of toucans in the world.

Toucan babies are born
with no feathers at all.
The mother and dad birds
both take care of the babies.
The babies might have three
or four brothers or sisters!

The most widely
recognized toucan is
the Toco Toucan.

Toucans are related
to the woodpecker.

Toucans like to live together in groups called flocks.

Toucans mainly travel among trees by hopping instead of flying.

A flock of toucans might be 5 or 6 birds together.

God made each rain forest
creature special.
He knows what they need
to live and grow.
He loves each one of these
special animals so much!

JUNGLE BEASTS

A jungle is usually a tropical forest with tall trees and other plants growing very thick and close together.

If a jungle is "tropical," it is usually hot and humid and can be very wet too.

God made all animals.

Some of the coolest animals

can be found in the jungle!

One animal in the hot jungle is the …

About half of all animal species on earth live in the jungle ... including mammals, birds, insects, amphibians, and reptiles.

It is believed more than two thirds of the world's plant species are found in the tropical rain forests.

PANTHERS

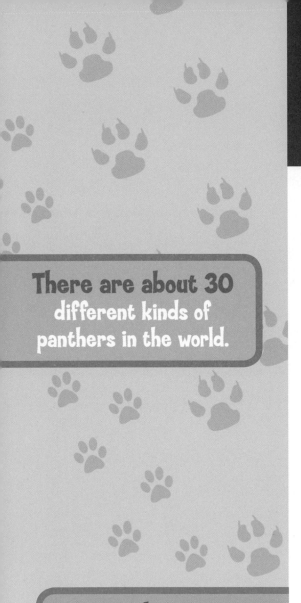

There are about 30 different kinds of panthers in the world.

Panthers are nocturnal. That means they move around and hunt mostly at night.

Panthers have lots of names.

They are sometimes called

pumas, mountain lions, or cougars.

Panthers usually live between 12-15 years in the wild.

A female panther is called a she-panther. A male is simply a panther.

An adult panther can weigh between 100 and 250 pounds.

Some favorite foods of the panther include deer, warthog, tapir, and antelope along with smaller species like birds and rabbits.

Panthers are really big cats.

These fast cats catch deer to eat.

Sometimes they even eat alligator!

They can leap up to 20 feet!
This helps them catch food
they spot from trees.

A panther's hind legs are both larger and slightly longer than those at the front which helps them jump far and fast.

Panthers are the strongest tree climbers in the cat world.

Panther cubs are born blind and do not open their eyes until they are nearly two weeks old.

Cubs won't leave their mother until they are nearly 2 years old.

A baby panther is called a cub. Cubs are as big as a full-grown house cat when they are born.

Another cool animal

in the hot jungle is the …

ANTEATER

The silky anteater is the size of a squirrel or cat.

The northern tamanduas live in the very dense forests of South and Central America.

There are four different kinds
of anteaters.

The giant anteater is best known
and really is giant.

They grow five to seven feet long.

They can weigh up to 100 pounds.

The southern
tamanduas
are also called
collared anteaters.

Baby anteaters
travel on their
mother's back until
they are about
1 year old.

The anteater uses sharp claws to help break open ant or termite hills they are looking in for food.

The anteater eats quickly, flicking its tongue up to 160 times per minute.

Their long snouts help them sniff out food because their eyesight is bad.

Anteaters can eat 30,000 ants
in one day.
Having a two-foot-long tongue helps!
Their tongues produce sticky saliva
which keeps insects from escaping.

Anteaters like to hunt for their food during the night.

Some anteaters sleep up to 15 hours a day.

But anteaters eat more than just ants. Termites are also on the menu. And if the anteater lives at a zoo, he might eat mashed fruit such as bananas and avocados.

There are thousands of different kinds of fruits that grow in the jungle, providing food. Common fruits like figs, oranges, pineapples, and bananas grow alongside unusual ones such as maracuja, acai, and the bacaba.

A common estimate is that about half of the world's animal species live in the rain forest/jungles.

Another fruit-loving animal

from the jungle is the …

ELEPHANT!

An elephant can live to be 70 years old!

Adult female and young elephants live in groups called herds.

Elephants can eat up to 5% of their body
weight in one day.

That can be up to 660 pounds
of grass, leaves, fruit, and bark.

And they might eat 18 hours a day!

Adult male elephants
like to either travel
alone or with groups
of other males.

Tusks are ivory
teeth that keep growing
through the elephant's
whole life.

A mother elephant is pregnant for about 22 months and when the baby elephant is born he weighs about 200 pounds.

Because of their huge size, other animals do not usually bother adult elephants.

The elephant is the largest animal that lives on land.

They can grow up to eleven feet tall and weigh 7,000 to 13,000 pounds.

That's more than a car weighs!

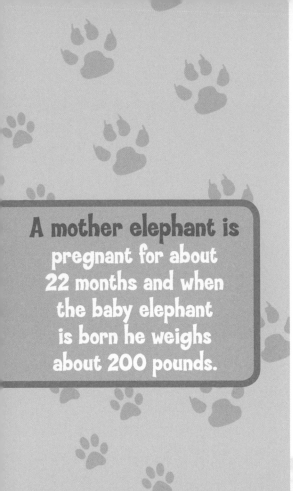

African elephants have "fingers"
at the end of their long trunks.
These help them pick things up.

An adult elephant's trunk can be up to 7 feet long.

An elephant's trunk is used for many jobs including to help pick things up, but it is really the nose of this huge animal.

There are two species of elephants—African and Asian elephants.

One way to tell the two species apart is African elephants have huge ears and Asian elephants have smaller ears.

Even though elephants have big ears, they have bad hearing!

But those big ears have a job!

Elephants flap their ears like fans
to help keep cool
in the hot jungle.

When elephants flap their ears, it can also be a sign of either joy or aggression.

Elephants use their trunks to help stay cool. They fill their trunks with water and spray themselves while in the super-hot sun. While they are wet, the elephants then sprinkle dust all over themselves, making their own kind of sunscreen!

Elephants have some very human qualities:

- They care for sick and wounded elephants in their herd or family.
- They are sad when another elephant dies.
- They remember friends and show happiness when they see them after a long time.
- They can hold grudges.

A much smaller jungle animal is the …

IGUANA

Iguanas are reptiles.

A reptile is a cold-blooded animal that has dry, scaly skin and usually its babies come from eggs. Some reptiles are lizards, snakes, and turtles.

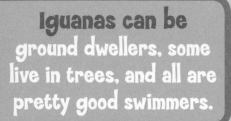

Iguanas can be ground dwellers, some live in trees, and all are pretty good swimmers.

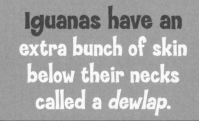

Iguanas have an extra bunch of skin below their necks called a *dewlap.*

There are many kinds of iguanas.

Some are the green iguana and

the lesser Antillean iguana.

Some iguanas are small

like the green iguana.

This kind makes a good pet.

They can live in aquariums or cages.

You have to buy heat lamps to keep pet iguanas warm.

They are cold-blooded, which means their temperature is around 85 degrees.

The dewlap helps iguanas regulate their temperature, which is helpful as they are cold-blooded and cannot control their body temperature automatically.

The dewlap also helps them communicate. The iguana will spread the dewlap wide to appear bigger and bob its head up and down so they appear scary.

The anole is the smallest member of the iguana family ... growing to only about 8 inches.

An iguana's tail can be about half the lizard's length!

Other iguanas grow up to 6½ feet long! That's longer than some basketball players are tall.

What do iguanas eat to get that big?

It is true that a healthy iguana might re-grow his tail if it breaks or falls off.

People in some parts of the world eat iguana meat.

Another name for vegetarian is herbivore.

There are some reptiles in the iguana family that will eat insects.

Iguanas are vegetarians.

Iguanas eat fruits, flowers, and leaves.

They love leafy vegetables such as spinach and kale.

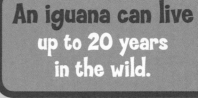

An iguana can live up to 20 years in the wild.

Iguanas have a "third eye" on the top of the head, a patch of pale, scaly skin that senses light (but does not see images).

Iguanas come in many different colors.

They can be brown, green, or even red.

This helps them hide from animals

that might want to eat them.

God made all animals.

He made animals with fur and
others with leathery skin.

And some of the coolest animals
can be found in the hot jungle!

POLAR PALS

When we say "polar regions" we are usually talking about the North and South Poles.

The North and South Poles have freezing conditions all the time. This means there is ice, snow, and very little vegetation growing.

God made many animals.

Some live where it is warm,

like the roadrunner.

Some live where it is very cold,

like the …

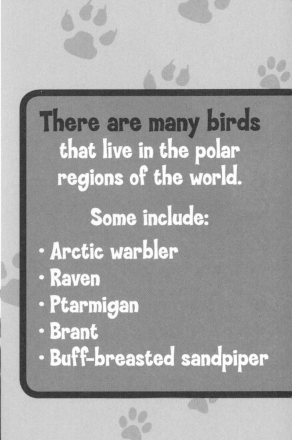

There are many birds that live in the polar regions of the world.

Some include:
- Arctic warbler
- Raven
- Ptarmigan
- Brant
- Buff-breasted sandpiper

No penguins live at the North Pole.

EMPEROR PENGUIN!

The emperor penguin lives

in Antarctica near the South Pole.

There are a total of 17 kinds of penguins in the world.

Emperor penguins can swim about 7.6 miles an hour!

Sometimes it can be 42° F below zero!

The water where they

swim and catch food

might be only 28° F!

That is colder than ice.

While swimming, Emperor penguins can dive very deep and stay underwater about 20 minutes.

Four layers of scale-like feathers protect penguins from icy winds and provide a waterproof coat.

The smallest penguin is the Little Blue Penguin, also called the Fairy Penguin. It can be about 16 inches tall and weigh 2 pounds.

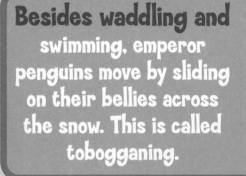

Besides waddling and swimming, emperor penguins move by sliding on their bellies across the snow. This is called tobogganing.

The emperor penguin is the biggest penguin—they can be four feet tall.

They might weigh 65 pounds.

These penguins cannot fly.

God made sure they are great swimmers

since they spend most of their

lives in the sea

looking for food like

krill and squid.

Penguins catch all their food under the water.

Emperor penguins drink seawater.

Mother emperor penguins lay one egg at a time.

Unlike most other birds, emperor penguins lay their eggs in the winter. Then the mother leaves the egg with the father and goes to find food for herself and the baby that will hatch.

Emperor penguins live in huge colonies.

While the father penguins take care of their babies, the colony works to keep everyone warm by staying close together.

Another kind of cold-weather bird that stays together is the …

Some types of penguins are:

- Chinstrap penguins
- Gentoo penguins
- Galapagos penguins
- Rockhopper penguins
- Yellow-eyed penguins
- Macaroni penguins

The Arctic tern is a relative of the sea gull.

ARCTIC TERN!

A group of arctic terns can also be called a flock.

Like penguins, most terns mate for life.

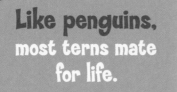

The arctic tern is a small bird that lives in large groups called colonies, just like penguins.

The tern can be 12 inches long and weigh two to four ounces. They eat mostly small fish they catch by diving down to the water.

The tern hovers over the water watching very closely to make sure its food is there before diving down to get the fish with its bill.

Some of the arctic tern's favorite foods are capelin, sand launae, sand eel, and small crustaceans.

The arctic tern is a long-distance flier that often returns to the place it was hatched.

The arctic tern may fly hundreds of miles in its lifetime.

Many birds fly south for the winter.

The arctic tern has the longest trip of any bird.

They breed in the Arctic tundra—the North Pole—and then fly to the edge of Antarctica for the winter.

That is over 21,750 miles—almost as many miles as the circumference of the earth!

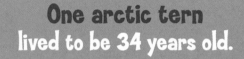

One arctic tern
lived to be **34** years old.

The mother arctic tern
lays 1-3 eggs and both
she and the father bird
care for them. The eggs
can be blue-white,
cream, green, or even
dark brown and speckled.

The arctic tern was once hunted so people could use their feathers to make hats.

Foxes, rats, raccoons, and weasels are predators of the tern and their eggs.

These special cold-weather birds travel with their colonies. Right before they take off, the whole colony gets very, very quiet … that is called "dread." Then, all of a sudden, they all take off together.

Terns work together in their colonies to defend their nests.

Terns help human fishermen catch more fish. When they see a group of terns hovering over water they know there is a school of fish in that area.

Polar bears are the largest land meat-eater in the world.

Polar bears are the largest bear of the bear family.

Another animal that loves the cold is the …

POLAR BEAR!

Polar bears have a keen sense of smell and use their sensitive lips and whiskers to explore objects.

In the wild, polar bears are estimated to live 25 to 30 years.

Polar bears most often like to be alone. The exception is when a mother bear is caring for her young.

Polar bears dog-paddle with their head and much of their back above the water.

Polar bears live in the Arctic.

They can be found in areas of Alaska,

Canada, Greenland, Norway,

and Russia.

They spend most of their lives in the sea hunting for seal, walruses, and other small water animals.

Polar bears do not drink water.

Polar bears' blubber helps them float while swimming.

Sometimes polar bears travel on ice floes looking for food and will occasionally get stranded on land far away from others.

Father polar bears are called boars.

Mothers are called sows.

They can grow to be ten feet long

and weigh 1,700 pounds!

Polar bear height:
average adult male
8.5 ft. (2.6 m)

Polar bear height:
average adult female
6.5 ft (2 m)

Polar bears technically do not hibernate but stay in their dens to either wait for their cubs' birth or to avoid terrible weather.

When a mother bear has cubs,

she usually has twins.

She builds a snow den and sleeps

all winter, waiting for her babies.

The father is active all year long.

Cubs stay with their mother for 2 to 3 years.

Fur grows on the bottoms of polar bear's paws to help protect them from the cold and to give better traction or grip on the ice.

The skin underneath a polar bear's white fur is black. This helps the bear soak up the warming rays of the sun.

God gave polar bears two layers of fur.

One layer is thick and woolly.

It is close to the skin and keeps the bear warm.

They also have hollow guard hairs. These stick up and protect the bear from getting wet.

These hairs are like clear straws (not white).

The white-looking coat camouflages polar bears in the snow and ice.

Sometimes when polar bears live in zoos that are in a warmer climate, they can have algae growing inside the hollow guard hairs of their fur. This makes them have a greenish tint to their fur.

The camouflage of the polar bear's white fur works so that the bears are better able to sneak up on their prey as they hunt.

An arctic fox has fur on the soles of its feet just like the polar bear, to keep their feet warm in the cold snow and ice.

These fox have a great sense of smell and excellent hearing.

Another Arctic animal that God gave great camouflage to is the …

ARCTIC FOX!

An adult arctic fox is about as big as a large cat.

It is said the arctic fox has the warmest fur of any mammal on earth.

The arctic fox is found in places like Northern Canada, Russia, Greenland, Iceland, and Alaska.

Some favorite foods the arctic fox eats are lemmings, voles, small birds, eggs, berries, and fish.

This special fox is found farther north than any other land mammal in the world.

Their fur is white in the winter
and turns gray-brown in
the summertime.
This is helpful if they want
to hide and also when they hunt.

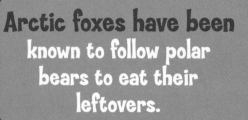

Arctic foxes have been known to follow polar bears to eat their leftovers.

These fox track their prey in their underground homes. When they hear something, they jump up and down, cracking through the top layer of snow and ice to reach the prey.

A male fox is called a reynard.

A mother fox is called a vixen,

and her babies are kits.

An arctic fox can live up to 15 years.

Female arctic foxes give birth each spring to a large litter of up to 14 kits, also called pups.

The tail of an arctic fox is also called a brush.

The fox's tail is about 35% of its total length.

God gave the foxes a big, bushy tail.

One way they use their tail is to keep warm.

When they go to sleep they tuck it around their feet and nose.

It also helps them change direction when they are running.

God is so good!

He makes sure that all of his

creatures have what they need

to live in the hot as well as

the very cold parts of the world.

CURIOUS CREATURES DOWN UNDER

God made everything everywhere.

He made where you are,

and he made a place called

Australia, which is sometimes

called Down Under.

Koalas inhabit the forests of eastern Australia.

Koalas smell like cough drops because of their diet of eucalyptus leaves!

God made some special animals that live Down Under.

One of them is the …

KOALA!

The word *koala* may come from an Aboriginal word meaning "no drink."

Although not considered endangered, 80% of the original koala habitat has been destroyed since Europeans settled in Australia.

Some joeys are about the size of a large jelly bean when they are born.

When joeys are born they are hairless, blind, and do not have ears.

The koala is sometimes called a koala bear.

It is not a bear.

The koala is a marsupial.

That means it has a pouch to carry its baby, called a joey.

A joey will live in its mother's pouch for about 7 months while it grows and develops more.

Koalas can be two to three feet long and weigh ten to thirty pounds.
They have gray or light brown fur and good paws for climbing.

On average, female koalas are smaller than males.

Koalas are picky eaters.

They eat only eucalyptus

leaves and do not drink water!

There are hundreds of kinds of eucalyptus but each koala has two or three favorites they eat all the time.

Koalas eat a little bit of dirt to help them better digest the leaves they eat.

Koalas are nocturnal.
That means they are active
at night.
Koalas love to live in groups
but they rest or sleep about
18 to 20 hours a day!

Koalas sometimes jump from tree to tree to get more leaves to eat.

Koalas mark their own territory by leaving scratches in the tree bark.

There are over 60 species of kangaroos in Australia.

A kangaroo gets most of the water it needs to survive from the greens it eats.

God made another Australian animal that lives on leaves. It does not need a lot of water. It is the …

KANGAROO!

When a kangaroo fights, it rears up and tries to use its forearms to grab the other kangaroo, making it look as though it is boxing.

Kangaroo fur is usually gray, brown, or reddish in color.

Kangaroos are found Down Under. They like to live in forests and grassy plains called savannas.

The kangaroo is the national symbol of Australia.

Kangaroos keep themselves cool by licking their forearms or panting.

Kangaroos wander around their home to find good food to eat.

They live in mobs.

Each mob has a male kangaroo in charge.

Kangaroos often communicate with their mob by thumping the ground with their strong feet.

A group of kangaroos can also be called a troop or court.

Some humans hunt kangaroos for food and the hides.

On average, kangaroos live in the wild for 6 to 8 years.

Kangaroos can grow to be

six feet tall and weigh 200 pounds!

They have strong tails to help

keep their balance

and muscular legs to jump and run.

When necessary, a kangaroo can swim.

Most kangaroos hunt for food at night and rest in the shade during the day.

Some kangaroos can run as fast as 25 miles an hour! Some jump ten feet into the air!

Kangaroos have one baby at a time. Their babies are called joeys. Joeys are born and then go into their mother's pouch and stay for about eight months!

A joey is about the size of a grain of rice when born.

Kangaroos cannot run backwards.

A male kangaroo is called a buck, boomer, jack, or old man. A female kangaroo is called a doe, flyer, or jill.

The red kangaroo is the largest marsupial in the world.

Besides thumping on the ground, kangaroos make grunting, coughing, hissing, and clicking noises to communicate.

Adult echidnas can be 13–17 inches long.

Adult echidnas can grow to be 6 to 14 pounds.

Another animal that God made for this special place is the …

ECHIDNA!

Although echidnas are considered common and widespread, they are protected by law in Australia.

Echidnas have predators such as goannas (large Australian monitor lizards), dingoes, foxes, feral cats, dogs, eagles, and Tasmanian devils.

To protect themselves, echidnas will often curl up into a ball and lie still until the threat is gone.

Sometimes they dig into the soil or under fallen limbs and wedge themselves in an opening, exposing their spines to the threat as well.

The echidna (e-kid´-na) is also called a spiny anteater.

God created them to look like a hedgehog or porcupine.

He put sharp spines on their skin so they can protect themselves.

Echidnas are not like a hedgehog or porcupine for a big reason. Echidnas are mammals that lay eggs and make milk for their babies!

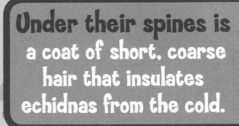

Under their spines is a coat of short, coarse hair that insulates echidnas from the cold.

A baby echidna is called a puggle.

Echidnas live all over Australia.

They like deserts, forests, and hills.

As long as they find their favorite foods—

ants and termites—they are happy.

Echidnas have been known to live for as long as 16 years in the wild.

An echidna uses its long sharp claws and short, sturdy limbs to dig into the soil and expose its prey.

Echidnas do not have teeth.

They catch their dinner with a sticky

tongue and crush the bugs before eating.

Echidnas are nocturnal

so they eat at night.

This is similar to another

animal Down Under, the …

Echidnas also live in **New Guinea.**

The echidna is a monotreme, which means that it is a mammal that lays eggs.

PLATYPUS!

A mother platypus will dig a very deep tunnel, called a nursery burrow, when she's ready to lay her eggs.

These burrows sometimes extend 100 feet (30 meters) from the water.

The platypus is another mammal that is special because it lays eggs to have babies and makes milk to feed them. Adult platypuses eat water bugs, shrimps, and worms.

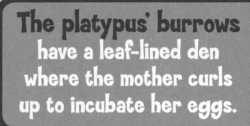

The platypus' burrows have a leaf-lined den where the mother curls up to incubate her eggs.

A platypus baby is about the size of a lima bean.

A platypus has webbed feet.

They look for food in the water at night, using their bill to search for their favorite foods.

Platypuses are called

duck-billed platypus because

they have long snouts.

It looks like a duck's bill.

They use it to help find food.

Their mouth has no teeth. Instead, a pad of rough skin near their throat grinds up food before swallowing.

The platypus brings its food to the surface of the water to eat.

When looking for food, platypuses can stay underwater for about two minutes.

Platypuses are eaten by a wide array of Australian predators, including dingoes, foxes, large snakes, and even eels.

Platypuses are about as big as a pet cat.

They have water-proof fur.

That is a good thing!

They live by freshwater and

love to swim and dive.

God gave the male platypus a small

spike on his back ankles.

It is poisonous and helps him

protect himself.

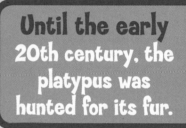

Until the early 20th century, the platypus was hunted for its fur.

A Good Question:
What is the difference between an animal being endangered and being threatened?

THREATENED species are the animals that could completely disappear from earth. There are different levels of how serious that can be.

ENDANGERED is one of the levels of being endangered.

God makes sure his special creatures can take care of themselves. Let's help his creatures all over the world stay safe!

The 3 levels of being threatened are:

Critically Endangered
—a species facing an extremely high risk of extinction (disappearing) in the wild.

Endangered
—a species considered to be facing a very high risk of extinction in the wild.

Vulnerable
—a species considered to be facing a high risk of extinction in the wild.

Subject Index

these other books about God's creation!

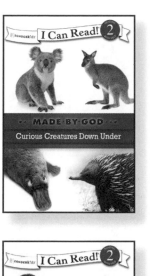

MADE BY GOD
Big Bugs, Little Bugs

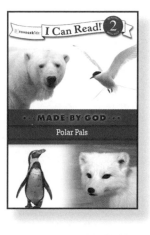

MADE BY GOD
Curious Creatures Down Under

MADE BY GOD
Polar Pals

MADE BY GOD
Barnyard Critters

MADE BY GOD
Forest Friends

MADE BY GOD
Jungle Beasts